Sparkleshark

A play

Philip Ridley

Samuel French — London
New York - Toronto - Hollywood

SPARKLESHARK

Sparkleshark was commissioned by the Royal National Theatre, London, for the BT National Connections Scheme for young people in 1997. The play was first performed at the Royal National Theatre on 15th July, 1997 by the Youth Lyric Theatre, Belfast:

Jake	Barum Jeffries
Polly	Nadine Shaker
Natasha	Tara Taylor
Carol	Rachel Lyndsay
Russell	Robert Davison
Buzz	Gordon Barr
Speed	John Gibson
Shane	Conor Ritchie
Finn	Jonathan Haveron

Director **Michelle Wiggins**
Assistant Director **Gordon Barr**

Subsequently performed at the Royal National Theatre, London, on 7th June, 1999 with the following cast:

Jake	Nitzan Sharron
Polly	Jody Watson
Natasha	Maggie Lloyd-Williams
Carol	Kellie Bright
Russell	Chiwetee Ejiofor
Buzz	Nicholas Aaron
Speed	Lee Oakes
Shane	Paul Sharma
Finn	Charlie J Watts

Directed by **Terry Johnson**
Designed by **Annie Gosney**
Lighting by **Steve Barnett**
Sound by **Neil Alexander**

COPYRIGHT INFORMATION

(See also page ii)

CHARACTERS

Jake
Polly
Natasha
Carol
Russell
Buzz
Speed
Shane
Finn

The action of the play takes place on the rooftop of a tower block

Time: a September afternoon. The present

For all the Jakes
of the World

"We won't use guns,
we won't use bombs,
we'll use the one thing we've got more of——
that's our minds."

(from *Mis-shapes* by Pulp)

SPARKLESHARK

The rooftop of a tower block in the East End of London. It is about 4.30 p.m. Mid-September. The weather is sunny

Many TV aerials and satellite dishes, a large puddle, discarded household furniture, a supermarket trolley, piles of rubbish and various scattered detritus. Some precarious metal steps lead from the main larger area of the roof up to a tiny platform. There's a doorway here, leading to the emergency stairs. This is the only entrance to the roof

Jake enters. He is fourteen years old, slightly built and clutching a satchel. He is wearing a well-worn, but still clean and tidy, school uniform and glasses (the left lens is cracked and the bridge held together by sticky tape). His hair is neatly cut

Jake makes his way down to the main area of the roof and sits in an old armchair. He is familiar and comfortable with these surroundings. It's a place he's been many times before—his secret hideaway. He takes a notebook from the satchel and reads, nodding and murmuring thoughtfully. Then he takes a pen from the inside pocket and writes

Jake Big ... fish! Big fish...! No, no. (*He tears the page from the notebook, screws it up and throws it aside. He starts pacing the roof and continues to write*) Glitter! Glitter piranha...! No, no.

Polly enters. She is fifteen years old and wearing the same kind of school uniform as Jake, although hers is obviously brand new (and has a skirt instead of trousers). Her hair is long, but held primly in place by an elastic band. She is clutching a tiny tool box

Polly watches Jake from the raised platform

Shark! Yes! Shark ... glitter... (*He turns and sees Polly. He lets out a yelp of surprise and drops his notebook*)

Loose pages flutter everywhere

Polly Oh, I'm sorry.

Jake starts picking up pages. Polly climbs down the metal steps and starts helping Jake

Jake Don't bother.
Polly No bother. (*She picks a page from the puddle*) This one's a bit soggy. Can't quite read——
Jake (*snatching it from her*) Don't! This is ... it's personal stuff. You can't just stroll up here and start reading things willy-nilly! Watch out! You're treading on one now! You should be in a circus with feet this size. What you doing up here anyway? This is *my* place! Go away!

Pause

Polly I've only got three things to say to you. One: what I'm doing up here is none of your business. Two: the roof is not your private property—unless, of course, you have a special clause in your rent book, which I doubt. And three: I find it strange that someone who can write such magical words has such a spiteful tongue in his head... Now, I've got something I need to do, then I'll be gone. In the interim, I'd be grateful if you didn't speak to me again. (*She goes to the satellite dish that's positioned on the edge of the roof. She opens the tool box, removes a screwdriver and—none too convincingly—starts fiddling*)

Pause

Jake Is it really magical?
Polly ...What?
Jake My writing.
Polly Bits.

Pause

Jake I... I was wondering whose dish that was.

Pause

   I'm Jake.
Polly I know.
Jake How?
Polly Oh, please... Your eyes! Use them! (*She indicates her school uniform*)
Jake You go to my school!
Polly Started last week.
Jake Haven't seen you.

Polly Not surprised. All you do is hide between those two big dustbins at the back of the playground.
Jake I like it there.
Polly But, surely, they're a bit ... well, smelly?
Jake Don't notice after a few deep breaths.
Finn (*off*) DATTSITPOLLLSUMMINSSSTARRTAPPENN!

Polly leans over the ledge

Polly All right, Finn! Tell me when it gets better.
Finn (*off*) KEEEPPOOOINNWHARRYARRROOOINNN!

Polly continues fiddling with the satellite dish

Jake That ... that voice! I've seen it—I mean, I've seen who it belongs to. He joined my class last week.
Polly That's my baby brother.
Jake Baby! But ... but he's huge! He grabbed two desks. One in each hand. And lifted them up. Above his head.
Polly I suppose even you would have to notice that.
Jake All the boys are scared of him. They call him the Monster.
Polly He's not a monster! Everyone calls him that. Everywhere he goes. But he's not. He's very gentle. Cries easily, if you must know.
Finn (*off*) GEEEINBEEERPOLLL!
Polly (*calling*) OK, Finn! (*To Jake*) It's getting better.
Jake You understand him?
Polly It might sound like a meaningless groan to you but—believe me—once you grasp the nuances, it's a very subtle form of communication.
Finn (*off*) BEEERPOLLBEEER!
Jake Subtle? That?
Polly Well, he's in a bad mood. Missing his favourite programme. That one with real life accidents. You know? Housewives setting themselves on fire with dodgy hairdryers.
Finn (*off*) NEEAREEAIRRPOLL!
Polly All right, Finn...! And everyone watches these programmes because they're supposed to be educational...
Jake But all they really want to see is someone's head getting sliced off by helicopter blades.
Polly Precisely.
Finn (*off*) DATSITPIKKERSPERRRFF!
Polly Thanks, Finn! That's it! He'll quieten now. Picture's perfect. Well, perfect as it'll ever be with this equipment. (*She starts packing up the tools etc.*) Dad got it cheap somewhere. I'm sure there's bits missing. And there

was no instruction manual. Haven't a clue what I'm doing really... You know anything about this sort of thing?

Jake All I know for sure is you've got to aim the dish at a satellite up there...

Polly Perhaps I should put it even higher—oh!

Jake What?

Polly A dead bird... Poor thing. Only a baby. Must have fallen from one of the nests. (*She peers closer at the dead bird*) All mauve and scarlet. Little yellow beak. Come and have a look.

Jake ...Rather not.

Polly Can't hurt you.

Jake Not that... I can be seen up there. By people in the football pitch.

Polly There's no-one in the football pitch.

Jake But there might be. Any minute now. If he sees me—oh, you won't understand.

Polly Try me.

Pause

Jake It's Russell.

Polly The turbo-dreambabe?

Jake Turbo *what*?

Polly That's what's written all over the toilets. "TICK HERE IF YOU THINK RUSSELL'S A TURBO-DREAMBABE."

Jake Bet the wall's covered.

Polly Everyone loves him.

Jake Love! I'll show you what your precious turbo-whatever has done— come here! Come on!

Polly goes to Jake

Feel! (*He points at the top of his head*)

Gingerly, Polly feels

Polly Oooo...

Jake An elbow did that. (*He rolls his trouser leg up*) And here!

Polly Very colourful.

Jake A foot! And look in my eyes. Does the left one look a little bloodshot?

Polly ...Yes.

Jake A fist!

Slight pause

Polly The turbo-dreambabe?

Jake Bingo! Hang on! You ticked! You like him!

Polly I don't know if I *like* him.

Jake You ticked!

Polly Yes, I ticked! The other day he took his shirt off in the playground and—yes, I admit—I felt a tingle.

Jake Animal!

Pause

Polly I'm sorry you're bullied. Russell is a nasty piece of work. It's like my mum used to say about Dad, "Sometimes the worst presents come in the nicest wrapping paper".

Slight pause

Jake Muscles! Who needs 'em? I don't want to do six thousand sit-ups a day. I don't care if I don't make people tingle.

Polly But you do! At least ... you do me.

Jake ...How?

Polly Your stories.

Jake How do you know about my stories?

Polly The other day ... when I was fixing up the satellite dish, I noticed... (*She takes several folded sheets from her pocket*) I'm sorry, I'm sorry, I know I shouldn't have. But ... oh, Jake, there's such wonderful things here. When I read them I ... I tingle as if a thousand Russells had revealed a thousand six-pack stomachs.

Pause

Jake You see the tower blocks? Over there! I imagine they're mountains! And other blocks—like this one—they can be Castles. Or mountains. Depending on the story. And ... those television aerials. They're a forest. I'm... I'm working on this new story. Don't know what it's about yet. But it'll have a Dragon in it. A Dragon with a head like ... like a giant piranha. Or shark. And its skin is all shiny. It sparkles. Like...

Polly Sequins!

Jake Exactly! I'm trying to work out the Dragon's name. I was thinking of something like ... Glittershark.

Polly Not quite right.

Slight pause

Sharktwinkle!

Jake No.

Natasha enters. She's fifteen years old and, although she's wearing the same kind of school uniform as Polly, her skirt is much shorter, the shirt is bright pink and unbuttoned to reveal some cleavage, and her shoes are platforms. Her make-up is heavy and her hair, though not long, screams for attention. In place of a satchel, she has a handbag covered with gold sequins

Natasha watches Jake and Polly

Polly Fishtwinkle—oh, no! That's terrible!

Polly and Jake turn and see Natasha. They let out a yelp of surprise

Natasha! How d'you get up here?
Natasha How did I? Oh, just my usual after-school abseiling. What d'ya mean, how did I get here, you silly cow? I walked up the bloody stairs. The last two flights need a bloody government health warning. Thought the boys' toilets at school were bad enough. (*She takes perfume from her handbag and sprays herself*)
Polly How d'you know I was up here, Natasha?
Natasha Your brother told me. Well, "told"'s a bit of an exaggeration. "Where's Polly, Finn?" "Uggghh!" (*She points up*) "What? She's in her bedroom?" "Uggghh!" (*She points up*) Finally, I work out it's either heaven or the roof. (*She takes lipstick and face compact from her handbag and starts to re-touch her make-up*) And, Polly—please don't take this the wrong way—but your brother stinks. The state of his hair should be punishable by law. And as for his breath! Phew! It could strip nail varnish at twenty paces. (*She starts to climb down the stairs*)
Polly What you doing, Natasha?
Natasha Oh, don't start that again! Give us a hand, Pol.

Polly helps Natasha down

Polly You should wear sensible shoes.
Natasha No girl wears shoes to be sensible.
Polly Wear them to get blisters, do they?
Natasha Beauty knows no pain. Now, Pol, quick. A word. (*She pulls Polly to one side*) Looks like we've got a yellow alert situation here.
Polly Yellow alert?
Natasha Don't play dumb, Little Missy. Cast your mind back. Your first day at school. You're standing alone in the playground. You're close to tears——

Polly I was not!

Natasha Who saved you from total cred oblivion?

Polly You made friends with me, if that's what you mean.

Natasha And you know why? Because under your totally naff surface, I detected the *real* you. The one who, by half-term, with my help and a make-over——

Polly I don't want a make-over!

Natasha Park your lips! What did I tell you on that first day? Be careful who you talk to. Ask me who's in, who's out. Did I say that?

Polly Yes.

Natasha So why the geek?

Polly He's not a geek! He's very nice.

Natasha Orange alert! Niceness has nothing to do with it. It's like saying someone with measles is nice. It don't matter. Geekiness is contagious! Now, let's get away from here pronto.

Polly I like Jake.

Natasha Red alert! Pol, you'll be hiding between the dustbins before the term's out.

Polly I don't care! He's my friend. And if you can't accept that, then ... well, you're not the deep, warm, sensitive, mature person I thought you were. Someone who's as beautiful inside as she is out.

Pause

Natasha ...Hiya, Jake.

Pause

I'm doing my hair different now. Had it cut since last term.

Polly Don't talk about yourself. Be interested in *him*.

Slight pause

Natasha So, Jake... What do *you* think about my hair?

Polly I didn't mean that.

Natasha Oh, I give up.

Jake Looked better before.

Slight pause

Your hair. When it was longer. Really suited you.

Polly Jake, I don't think——

Natasha Let him finish.

Slight pause

Jake Every day you'd do it slightly different. Sometimes swept this way. Sometimes that. And no matter what style, it always looked ... oh, so perfect. A real work of art. The effort that went into that.

Natasha Hours, believe me.

Jake And you wore hairclips—my favourite! The one with yellow flowers.

Natasha My favourite too. Still got it. (*She searches in her handbag*)

Jake But with shorter hair ... it's like you've lost part of you. And your make-up's different.

Polly Stop flirting.

Natasha He ain't flirting. He's talking like one of the girls. What's more, he's the only one who's had the guts to be honest. My hair was better longer—— (*She finds the hairclip*) Jake?

Jake That's the one.

Natasha Won't suit me now.

Slight pause

You have it, Pol.

Polly ...Me?

Jake It'd suit you.

Natasha The voice of an expert.

Polly (*taking the hairclip*) Oh, Tasha, you know I can't...

Natasha There's nothing wrong with making the most of yourself, Pol.

Slight pause

You've got to ... express yourself now and then. Not bottle everything up. Otherwise ... you're gonna explode.

Jake It's just a hairclip.

Polly Try telling my dad that.

Natasha Dads! Dads! Dads! What've I told you, Pol? You mustn't let it bother you. Water off a duck's back. Just like mine.

Jake What's wrong with your dad?

Slight pause

Natasha ...Hardly says a word to me.

Jake Why?

Natasha Just doesn't ... like me any more, I guess. If I walk in the room he looks right through me. Or worse—like I've got a dog turd smeared on my forehead Oh, I know what he's thinking. What he thinks of me... You know I was in hospital last term. Just before the summer holidays. A whole week. Guess how many times Dad visited…

Slight pause

Spilt milk. Been there. Seen it. Boohooed that!

Carol enters. She is fourteen years old and, although she's wearing her school uniform in the same way as Natasha—short skirt, coloured shirt (lemon), platforms, gold handbag, etc., she can't quite pull it off. Nothing seems to fit her properly and, even if it did, the awkwardness and self-consciousness would remain

Carol's breathless and clings to the rail for support

Carol! I thought I told you to wait downstairs, Little Missy.
Carol Didn't say. Wait a million. Years though. Did ya? Honestly, Pol, I can put up. With your brother breathing last night's curry. I can even put up with his Richter scale seven farts. But when he starts setting fire to them— well, I'm outa there. What you doing up here anyway? (*She sees Jake*) Yellow alert! Geek!
Polly Don't call him that!
Carol Orange alert!
Polly He's my friend!
Carol Red alert!
Natasha And mine!

Slight pause

Carol Hiya, Jake. (*She starts to negotiate descending the steps*)
Natasha Leave us alone, Carol.
Polly Maybe we should all go.
Natasha Don't you dare, Polly. I was just beginning to enjoy myself—Carol, sling your bloody hook!
Carol I was your friend first! Before her! Help me down.

Slight pause

Don't leave me out.
Natasha Clear off!

Carol starts to cry. Pause. Jake goes to Carol. He helps her down

On your head be it, Jake.

Carol has now reached the roof

The level of conversation's gonna drop faster than Carol's knickers in the boys' toilets.

Carol Why you such a bloody bitch all the time?

Natasha You make me! Bloody following me everywhere. Everything I do, you copy. You bloody wannabe. I buy platforms, so do you.

Carol You didn't bloody invent platforms!

Natasha (*indicating her handbag*) I buy this. The very next day—oh, surprise, surprise.

Carol They were in a sale!

Natasha I wear a coloured shirt——

Carol Mine's citrus lemon!

Natasha Because they ran out of frosty pink. You even cut your hair 'cos I did.

Carol I was thinking of this for ages!

Natasha Liar!

Carol is by Polly's satellite dish now

Polly Mind the dish there, Carol.

Carol Tell me this, Miss All That. If you're so bloody special, why did Shane dump you?

Natasha Shane didn't dump me.

Polly Who's Shane?

Jake He was expelled last year. Why did Shane dump you?

Natasha He didn't. I dumped him.

Carol Then why the Richter scale eight boohoos?

Natasha The boohoos weren't for him.

Carol Not what you told me.

Natasha Think I'd tell you the truth, Little Miss Internet?

Jake Why would you dump someone like Shane? He's so … you know.

Natasha Oh, yeah, I know. Shane the Brooding. Shane the Cool. Shane the Let's-Paint-My-Bedroom-Black. Shane the Let's-Stick-A-Compass-In-My-Palm-Whenever-I'm-Fed-Up. Oh, honestly! Sound like me?

Carol You said you loved it.

Natasha Boyfriend stuff is complicated. You won't understand till you get one.

Carol I've got a boyfriend!

Natasha Tonsil hockey with Russell is not having a boyfriend.

Carol He can't take his eyes off me.

Natasha For chrissakes, Carol, don't you know anything? Listen, if you go to a party, you wanna know what boy fancies you? I mean, really, really

fancies you? It's the one *not* looking at you. "Can't keep his eyes off me!"
Jesus! Shall I tell you what your precious Russell told wonderful, brooding
Shane kissing you was? Charity!

Carol Liar!

Natasha Ask him yourself.

Carol I will! (*She leans over the edge of the roof*) Russell!

Jake Don't!

Natasha She's joking.

Carol (*calling*) Up here! With Natasha!

Jake She's not! He plays down there!

Polly The football pitch!

Carol He's coming!

Jake Buzz and Speed will be with him.

Polly Hide, Jake.

Jake starts looking for a hiding place

Carol (*to Natasha*) And Shane!

Natasha What?

Carol Shane's with him!

Natasha looks over the edge

Natasha Oh, my God.

Carol giggles excitedly

    Polly! It's Shane!

Jake is unable to find a hiding place

Polly Behind me, Jake! Quick!

Jake gets behind Polly

    Tasha, we need your help! Quick!

Natasha …What?

Polly We need to hide Jake. Russell will——

Jake Kill me!

Natasha (*to Carol*) This is all your bloody fault, Little Missy.

Polly Quick!

Natasha runs to stand beside Polly

Carol What's going on?
Polly Closer, Tasha—Carol, we need you too. Quick! Or do you want to see Jake hurt?
Carol Hurt? No.
Polly Hurry!

Carol rushes to join Polly and Natasha. Jake hides behind them

Close up, Carol. No gaps!

Russell enters. He is fifteen years old, glossily good-looking, with a defined, hard body, created to flaunt. His school uniform (which would have been the same as Jake's) has been reduced to trousers and shirt, the latter being worn untucked, unbuttoned to reveal his chest, and with the sleeves rolled up. Instead of shoes, he's wearing trainers

Russell (*in the voice of a sports commentator*) "The winner! Russell the Love Muscle adds Gold Medal for Tower Block Climbing to his long list of trophies. Is there any stopping this sex-machine, babe-magnet?" (*He calls down the stairs*) Come on, you two. Hear them panting down there? Pathetic. But, girls, feast your eyes! Am I breathless?
Girls ...No.
Russell Sweating?
Girls ...No.
Russell Tired?
Girls ...No.
Russell Do not adjust your sets, girls. You are witnessing perfection. Look at you! Too dazzled to move. "The crowd cheers at this spunky, funky, hard-bod hunky. Women are throwing flowers. He blows one a kiss! She faints——"

Buzz and Speed enter. They are fourteen years old and wearing the reduced school uniform favoured by Russell, although their shirts are not unbuttoned. They are both shorter than Russell and, while not unattractive, lack the arrogant dazzle that makes Russell the natural leader. Both Buzz and Speed are carrying very full sports bags instead of satchels. Buzz is carrying an extra one which, presumably, belongs to Russell. This extra weight has no doubt contributed to their breathless condition

Talk about fainting! Pathetic or what?
Buzz He kept pushing me, Russ.
Speed He got in the way, Russ.
Buzz I'm carrying your bag, Russ.

Speed He used it to trip me, Russ.

Russell Out of the way, losers. Time to greet the fans. (*He jumps to the main area of the roof*) I know what you're thinking, girls. Why can't my hair shine like his? And as for his eyelashes—they're wasted on a bloke! Don't blame me. I was born with these gifts. Others—I worked at! (*He lifts his shirt to reveal his stomach*)

Carol lets out an involuntary squeal

Know what these muscles are called?

Slight pause

Horny as hell!

Buzz and Speed go to descend the metal stairs

You two! Jump like me! A man!

Buzz and Speed stand on the edge of the raised area, psyching themselves to jump. They are teetering, visibly wary and nervous

Watchya, Natasha. All right?

Natasha Fine.

Russell Avoiding us lately?

Natasha Why should I?

Russell Our Shane-boy.

Natasha Ancient history.

Russell Exactly what I just said. When Shane heard what's-her-face call you were up here. "Come up", I said. "Let bygones be bygones. So you split up! No big deal. What's it mean—not twiddling with each other's rude bits anymore?" (*To Buzz and Speed*) Jump, you two!

Buzz Stop calling us "you two"!

Speed We've got names.

Shane enters. He is sixteen years old and wearing black leather trousers, boots, red silk shirt—unbuttoned to reveal a razorblade necklace, a black jacket and sunglasses. His hair is longish and well groomed

Without missing a beat, Shane pushes Buzz and Speed. They fall awkwardly to the lower level. Polly, Natasha and Carol gasp. Russell bursts out laughing

Russell Nice one, Shane!

Buzz Bloody stupid, that!
Speed Could have broken me neck!
Russell Shut up, you two!

Shane sits at the top of the metal steps. Pause

Natasha Hiya, Shane.

Pause

How's it going?

Pause

Have a good summer?

Shane still doesn't respond. Pause

Carol Russell! When you kissed me. Remember?
Russell No.
Carol Yes, you do.
Russell If you say so.
Carol Natasha said that ... well, said you said. Said you said to Shane——
Russell Said what, for chrissakes?
Carol Said ... it was charity.

Buzz and Speed start laughing

Stop it! Stop it!
Natasha Belt up, you scrotums!

Buzz and Speed stop laughing

Russell Well, to be honest with you—what's your name again?
Natasha Carol. Her name's Carol.
Russell Well, Carol, it's probably true. But let me explain. I am a dreamboat.
You are not. Now, when a dreamboat kisses a dreamboat challenged
person—it's always charity. This ain't a bad thing. I'm giving you
something that—in normal circumstances—you wouldn't stand a hope in
hell of getting. Don't tell me you didn't like the kiss.
Carol ...No. I mean, yes!
Russell Would you like another smackeroonie?
Natasha Control yourself, Carol.
Russell Come here.

Polly Don't move!

Carol is whimpering at the back of her throat

Russell Oh, Carol! My tongue! It'll go deep enough to taste your cornflakes.

Suddenly, Carol can resist no more and rushes at Russell. Immediately, Buzz and Speed get a glimpse of Jake

Buzz Geek alert!
Speed Geek alert!
Russell What? Where? Well, well, well, hiding behind the girls. How pathetic. How ... one hundred percent...
Russell ⎫
Buzz ⎬ (*together*) Geek!
Speed ⎭
Carol Where's my kiss?
Russell Get him, you two!

Buzz and Speed go to grab Jake. Jake runs. Buzz and Speed chase

Jake Help!
Polly Leave him!
Natasha Don't, Russ!
Carol Where's my bloody kiss?

Buzz and Speed catch Jake

Jake Help!
Buzz Kick him, Russ!
Speed Punch him, Russ!
Russell I've got a better idea. Let's dangle him over the edge.
Buzz Wicked!
Speed Awesome!
Jake Polly! Help me!

Buzz and Speed take Jake to the edge of the roof

Polly He's done nothing to you!
Jake Natasha! Help!
Natasha Stop it, Russ! Stop! Shane—tell him!
Carol My kiss!
Russell Shut up about your bloody kiss! Who'd kiss you anyway? Like dangling your tongue in a dustbin. Right, Shane?

Carol You bloody ... git! You! You liar! You——
Jake Carol!
Carol Let him go!
Russell Hey, Shane! You should see his face! All scared and... He's pulling
   Buzz's hair! Ha! A geek with cheek!
Speed He's pulling *my* hair!
Buzz I'm Buzz.
Speed I'm Speed.
Russell Don't get touchy now, you two—lift him!

Buzz and Speed lift Jake

Jake Nooooo!
Polly Stop!
Carol Stop!
Natasha You're gonna really hurt him.
Russell Trying my best.
Natasha Shane!
Polly You can't! Please! He ... he was telling us a story. Wasn't he, Tasha?
Natasha ...What? Yeah! A good story.
Polly We ... we want to know the end.
Russell I hate stories.
Jake Help! Help!
Natasha Shane! Tell him! Please!

Slight pause

Russell What's it to be, Shane? Dangle or story?

Pause

Shane ...Story.
Russell But, Shane——
Natasha You heard!

Slight pause. Buzz and Speed put Jake down. Pause

Russell So?

Pause

Polly It... It was about this Princess, wasn't it, Jake? Am I right? Yes? This
   Princess. What happened, Jake?

Slight pause

That's right! Yes! She lived in a Castle. Well, I suppose all Princesses live
in Castles, don't they?

Natasha Wouldn't be seen without one.

Carol No way.

Slight pause

Polly And this Princess ... she lived in a Castle with her father.

Natasha The King, right?

Polly Exactly, Natasha! Thank you for reminding me. The Princess lived in
a Castle with her father. Who was indeed the King.

Russell Bloody rivetting this! Now, don't tell me. Her mother was, indeed,
the Queen.

Polly No. The Princess didn't have a mother. She died——

Russell At childbirth! Boring! Shane! Let's dangle the geek! He's not even
telling it.

Natasha The Queen had been murdered, if you must know.

Pause

Very nastily.

Slight pause

Horribly.

Buzz ...How?

Speed Yeah. How?

Polly One day ... the Castle was attacked. By the King's enemies. The
kingdom had been at war for a long time.

Speed The King should have been prepared then.

Polly Well ... yes. He was. Usually. The King was a great soldier.

Buzz So how come the enemy surprised him?

Natasha ...The baby Princess.

Carol The Castle was celebrating. Right?

Polly Exactly right, Carol. It was the day for celebrating the birth of the
Princess! A holiday for everyone. The Castle was full of food and music
and flowers.

Buzz A good ol' booze up.

Speed Peanuts and sausages on sticks.

Carol Everyone strutting their funky stuff!

Natasha And that's when the enemy attacked!

Buzz Bet the Castle was slaughtered.

Polly The King was too good a soldier for that. In fact, the King defeated the enemy that day!

Buzz But the Queen!

Speed What happened to her?

Polly She was shot in the heart with a single arrow.

Pause

And then ... her head was chopped off.

Pause

And then ... her head was eaten by a hungry pig.

Buzz Wicked!

Speed Awesome!

Carol I feel a bit sick.

Polly After that ... the King never let his defences down again. Am I getting this right, Jake? The King banned pleasure from the Castle.

Buzz What? No telly?

Russell Wouldn't be telly in those days.

Polly No dancing. No singing. No flowers. Nothing pretty or frivolous at all! He thought these things would turn the Princess weak.

Russell (*to Buzz and Speed*) Like you two!

Polly And, as she had to rule after him one day, and possibly fight many battles, he had to train her to be strong. Right, Jake?

Jake nods and murmurs. Slight pause

The King made the Princess wear a simple dress. And only one colour ... black!

Carol Not even citrus lemon?

Polly No.

Natasha I bet her shoes were sensible too.

Polly Very sensible. And guess what she had to drink...? Vinegar!

Buzz Disgusting!

Polly And eat...? Plain bread!

Speed No butter?

Polly No.

Buzz What about margarine?

Polly No! Nothing! The King forbade it! And then, one night...

Jake thumps the floor

What? A thump...? Yes! That's it. I remember now. The Princess heard something thump against her window.

Buzz What?

Polly A bird. (*She gets the dead bird*)

Speed Is it dead?

Polly Its neck's broken.

Buzz Let's see.

Speed Let's see.

Carol She buries it!

Polly In a secret corner of the Castle.

Buzz Why do girls bury things?

Speed Instead of cutting them up?

Jake ...There's something inside the bird.

Polly What, Jake?

Buzz Yeah, what?

Speed What?

Carol What?

Slight pause

Jake ...A flower seed.

Polly Of course. The bird's dinner! So, when the bird is buried—the seed grows! And next summer—— (*She takes the hairclip from her pocket*) Look! I'm going to wear it in my hair.

Speed How'd you do that?

Buzz Don't let the King see.

Polly Too late!

Carol Yellow alert.

Polly The Princess says, "I'm sorry, Dad! Please! It's just a flower. Please— ahhh!"

Speed What's happened?

Polly He's ... he's hit me.

Russell Bully!

Slight pause

Polly "What's that, Dad? Oh, no! No!"

Carol What's he say?

Buzz What?

Speed What?

Polly ...He doesn't want a daughter like me.

Natasha No!

Jake You're banished!

Slight pause

Polly I leave the Castle. (*She walks around the roof*) And for a while ...
there's nothing. I don't know where I'm going. Just ... a wasteland. I walk
and walk. And then—yes!—I find a forest!

Jake She plants her flower.

Polly It's full of seeds. (*She buries the hairclip beneath some rubbish*)

Jake And one year later...

Polly Hundreds of flowers!

Jake The following year!

Polly Thousands!

Jake The next!

Polly Millions! Look at them! Millions of yellow flowers! As far as the eye
can see! So beautiful. And I'm... I'm so happy here in the forest of a million
yellow flowers. Smell them! And what's that? There! Look! In the lake!
(*She points at the puddle*) Dolphins! Splashing and playing together. Oh,
yes! Yes!

Pause

Jake And then, one day, a Prince arrives.

Buzz Me!

Speed No! Me!

Jake The Prince is the most handsome man in all the land.

Russell Someone call my name?

Buzz I said it first.

Speed No! I did.

Russell Shut it, you two!

Jake gets the supermarket trolley and wheels it in front of Russell

Jake The Prince rode a chariot.

Russell You must be bloody joking!

Jake Said the Prince. Because he was strong and proud. He thought he should
walk everywhere. But he also knew that riding in ... the solid gold chariot
was an honour. An honour only given to true heroes.

Slight pause. Russell looks at Shane. Shane indicates he should get in

Russell Shane?

*Shane indicates Russell should get in again. Slight pause. Russell gets in the
supermarket trolley*

Where's my bloody horses then?

Everyone looks at Buzz and Speed

Buzz No way!
Speed No way!
Russell Shane?

Slight pause. Shane indicates Buzz and Speed should pull the trolley. Buzz and Speed grab hold of it

Gee up, Lightning! Gee up, Ned!
Buzz Hang on a minute! Who's Ned?
Russell You.
Buzz Oh, no! If he's Lightning, I ain't going to be called Ned. You can stuff that up your——
Jake Thunder!

Slight pause

Russell Gee up, Thunder and Lightning!
Buzz That's more like it, yeah.

Buzz and Speed pull the trolley

Russell Faster! Come on, you two!

Buzz and Speed pull the trolley round and round

Faster! Faster!

Buzz and Speed pull the trolley faster

Faster!
Speed That's it! I've had enough!
Jake The horses were exhausted, so the Prince—who was as kind and understanding as he was handsome—let them rest by a lake in the middle of the forest.

Slight pause. Buzz and Speed pull the trolley to the puddle

And then ... the Princess came across the travellers.
Polly Who are you?

Speed Lightning!

Russell She's talking to me, you pillock! You're a bloody horse! Watchya!
I'm a Prince.

Polly Beautiful.

Russell I work out.

Polly Not you. My forest. Look! A million yellow flowers.

Jake But, as far as the Prince was concerned, the Princess was more beautiful
than all the flowers put together.

Slight pause

Polly Why are you looking at me like that?

Russell ...Like what?

Polly Like there's something you want to say.

Pause

Oh, I know it's difficult. For a Prince like you, I mean. To say things ...
gentle things. You've had to be strong and brave all your life. As hard as
your horny-as-hell stomach. But you can say them to me, you know.

Slight pause

Do you think I'm beautiful?

Russell ...Not bad.

Polly Do you want me to leave my forest and live with you in your Castle?

Buzz Go for it, Russ!

Speed Yeah!

Russell ...I'm easy.

Slight pause

All right. Yeah. I wouldn't mind.

Polly But, Prince, my forest is so beautiful. How can I leave it? Even for a
Love Muscle like you?

Russell You're ... you're playing bloody games with me! I never liked you
in the first place—Shane!

Polly Don't go!

Russell stops. Slight pause

Jake The Princess could see the Prince was upset. She knew he didn't mean
what he was saying. So ... she offered him a challenge.

Slight pause

Polly Prince! There is ... something inside me that tingles for you. Honestly.
  I can't explain it. I'd like to give you a chance—or me a chance.
Russell ...What?
Polly Find me something more beautiful than a million yellow flowers. If
  you can do that, I will follow you anywhere.
Jake So the Prince searched.

Slight pause

  The Prince looks!

Russell looks at Shane. Shane nods. Slight pause

Polly Please do it, Prince.

Russell searches the roof. He finds an old shoe and takes it to Polly

  The most beautiful shoe ever made. Decorated with rubies and diamonds
  and stitched with gold thread... Beautiful. But not beautiful enough.

*Slight pause. Russell throws the shoe aside. He searches the roof once more.
He finds an old baseball cap and takes it to Polly*

Russell This is a crown! Right? It's made of platinum. It's decorated with
  a trillion bloody diamonds. Beautiful or what?
Polly Beautiful. But not beautiful enough.
Russell (*throwing the cap aside*) Bloody hell——
Buzz Go to a Witch.
Speed Yeah! Wicked! Ask a Witch.

All look at Natasha

Natasha Well, that's bloody typical!

Slight pause

  Come on, then. What you waiting for?

Russell goes to Natasha

  Hiya, Prince. So you've got to find——

Russell I ain't told you yet!
Natasha I'm a bloody Witch, dickhead!

Pause

So... Little Miss Flower Power wants you to find something more
beautiful than a million yellow flowers. I can do that. But first ... you gotta
pay.
Russell How much?
Natasha Not money, you turbo-dreambabe. A kiss. A big smackeroo.
Mouth open. Tongue in lung.
Russell What? Here? In front of ... everyone?
Natasha But we're in my own witchy hovel.

Russell looks at Shane, then back at Natasha

I'm waiting.

*Russell kisses Natasha. It grows increasingly passionate. Carol slaps at
Russell*

Carol Stop it! You sod! Why her?
Russell Hey! What's your problem?
Carol It's not fair——
Natasha Calm down! Jesus! Get a grip!

Carol calms

You make yourself look a bloody idiot sometimes. Then wonder why
everyone's laughing at you. It's humiliating. You should be bloody
ashamed. Hear me? Ashamed.

Slight pause

You'll have to forgive my little creature, Prince.
Russell Little creature?
Natasha ...My pet frog.

Slight pause

Carol ...Croak, croak.
Natasha And now, Prince. I'll grant your wish. (*She takes the perfume from
her handbag*) This is my most magic potion. One spray of this and the
Princess will quiver and swoon.

Russell What do you think I am? (*He turns to face Shane*) Shane?

Natasha sprays the perfume on Russell

  Stop!
Natasha Done now!

Buzz and Speed laugh

Russell It's the knackers yard for you two!
Polly Mmmm ... what's that smell?

Slight pause. Russell goes to Polly

  Very, very beautiful. But ... a bit too fruity for my taste.
Russell That's it! Enough!
Shane You shouldn't have trusted the Witch.
Russell *You* bloody did!
Shane Her magic potion worked then——
Jake Said the Wizard.

Pause

Shane ...Let me tell you about the Witch.

Slight pause

  A million years ago I met her. On a planet far away. She was a powerful
  sorceress then. Her magic potion was the most potent in the universe.
  Savage monsters could be tamed with one whiff. I was tamed.

Slight pause

  And then, one day, she refused to answer when I called her name. I
  screamed so loud stars became supernova.

Slight pause

  She has spent a million years avoiding me. Fleeing each planet as I arrive.
  I've been trying to work out why she loved me so much one day ... then,
  the next, not at all.

Slight pause

An egg.
Natasha Wh-what?

Slight pause

Jake A Dragon's egg.
Polly A Dragon's egg, yes!
Buzz Wicked!
Speed Awesome!
Carol What about it?

Slight pause

Jake ...The Wizard told the Prince about this Dragon. It lives in the mountain——
Polly I've heard about this Dragon. It's got jaws like a shark.
Jake And scales like sequins.
Polly And this Dragon—yes, of course!—it lays eggs.
Jake ⎤
Polly ⎦ (*together*) Eggs more beautiful than a million yellow flowers!

Slight pause

Shane Go to the mountain. Find the Dragon's egg. The Princess will be yours.
Buzz But ... won't there be two Dragons?
Speed A mum and a dad?
Jake It's an hermaphrodite Dragon.

Slight pause

Half boy, half girl.
Russell Relative of yours, Jake?
Jake It's a ferocious Dragon. It might be covered with sequins. But each sequin is as sharp as a razor blade.

Slight pause

Be careful, Prince.

Pause

Russell (*in a sports commentator voice*) "The Prince faces the challenge without fear. Is this the bravest man on earth or what? In a few incredible strides he scales the heights of the mountain." (*He climbs the metal stairs*) "It's freezing cold, but is the Prince shivering? No! He's not even wearing protective clothing. Is this man mortal, we have to ask ourselves! And there... Is it? Yes! I believe it is! He's found it! Easy!" (*He takes a football from his sports bag*) The Dragon's egg!

Shane The cold must be making the Prince hallucinate.

Pause

Russell "Undeterred, the turbo-dreambabe of a Prince searches again! What stamina! What grit! And now... Yes!" (*He lifts an old lampshade in the air*) The Dragon's egg!

Shane Hallucination.

Russell What then, for chrissakes?

Carol I'll help you! Yeah, me, the frog! You see, ever since you came to visit the Witch... I've been thinking about you. Richter scale eight crush. Can't help it. Don't understand it—before you say anything, I don't want a kiss. You don't fancy frogs. That's your problem. No reason to hate you. I'll find a frog of my own to snog when this is over.

Speed Croak!

Carol In your dreams!

Slight pause

In the meantime, there's the egg. (*She points*)

Russell Where?

Carol There!

Russell But what? Where?

Pause

Ah! I get it! Hallucination and all that. Imagination. Nice one... Yes! I see it! There! More beautiful than anything I ever thought I'd find.

Shane Describe it.

Slight pause

Russell It's in a nest. A huge nest. Trees instead of twigs. All twisted and broken together. Bushes instead of leaves...

Slight pause

The egg's in the middle. Very big! Sparkling with a million colours... I'm

climbing into the nest now... Insects buzz all round me... Wood cracks at
my feet... (*He mimes picking up the egg*) The Princess will be mine!
Buzz Yeah.
Speed Yeah.
Russell Thank you, frog.
Natasha Back in your pond, frog!
Carol You made me a frog! With the last Witch I served I was a cat! A sleek,
graceful cat with big green eyes. Yes, I change depending on who I'm with.
But it's the Witch that changes me. You hear that? I don't change myself.
I hate you for changing me into a frog. I hate you for laughing because
someone ... someone I love thinks I'm ugly.
Russell I don't think you're ugly.
Carol They why didn't you kiss me?
Russell Because I don't feel ... like that towards you. Don't mean I think
you're ugly. We can be—well, you know.
Carol What?
Russell You know.
Carol No. What?
Russell ...Well, we don't have to be enemies.

Slight pause

Jake And look! You're not a frog any more. You're a beautiful nightingale.
Carol A nightingale! Princess! Look what the Prince has found!
Russell The Dragon's egg!
Polly Take me to your Castle.
Buzz Go on, my son!
Speed Yeah!
Jake And the Prince and Princess were married!

*Polly and Russell parade hand in hand. Everyone, except Natasha, cheers
and claps. Buzz and Speed tear bits of paper up and throw them as confetti*

Natasha It's not over!

The celebration dies down

What? You think it's that bloody easy. Find a beautiful egg and all live
happily ever after—you make me puke!
Shane ...What you going to do?

Slight pause

Natasha Curse the egg!

Russell What curse?

Natasha The egg's beauty! It'll be too much for the Princess! It'll ... hypnotise her. Take over her life!

Pause

Do it!

Slight pause

Do it!

Slight pause. Polly sits in the armchair and stares in front of her

Polly Oh, the colours! The lights! The shapes!

Russell goes to Shane

Russell I've got a feeling that Witch has cursed the egg.
Shane I think you're right.
Russell You're a bloody Wizard. Break the spell.
Shane It's too powerful for me.
Russell What now?
Shane Does the Princess love you?
Russell Who knows?
Shane Do you love her?
Russell I ... well...
Shane *Could* you love her?
Russell ...Probably.
Shane Then you must go to her. Every day. Tell her how much she means to you. Perhaps, in time, she will love you back. Who knows? This love might break the spell.
Russell You don't sound too sure.
Shane I'm not.

Slight pause

Do it.

Russell goes to Polly

Russell Wotchya, Princess. You know, I've been thinking about you ... a lot. You know? In my mind! You pop into it.

Pause

I've never spoken to anyone like this before——

Buzz and Speed giggle

Shut up, you two. This is important. Help or clear off!
Buzz Sorry, Russ.
Speed Sorry, Russ.

Slight pause

Russell I've seen lots of nasty things, Princess. In ... battles. You know? It's hard out there. Tough. I've seen friends really hurt. You know what I'm saying? Out there—I've done what ... what a Prince had to do. Otherwise ... well, he'll never be King.

Pause

Princess ... please ... listen to me. I'm trying...
Polly Oh, Prince.
Jake It's cracking!
Shane The egg!
Polly It mustn't hatch! No! No! (*She picks up the imaginary egg and starts to run*)
Jake Catch her!

Russell, Buzz and Speed chase after her. Everyone is crying out, adding to the general pandemonium

Russell Stop!
Shane Don't panic!
Buzz It's all right!
Speed Don't worry!
Polly The egg mustn't break!
Buzz She's lost it!
Speed Gone doolally.
Carol Princess!
Jake Mind the edge!

Polly is standing by her satellite dish now

Polly I hate you! Hate what you've done to my beautiful egg! You monster! Hate you!

Buzz Who's she talking to?
Speed The baby Dragon.
Carol It's hatched.
Buzz It's at her feet.
Shane She's going to kill it!
Natasha No!
Russell No!
Carol No!
Buzz No!
Speed No!

Natasha rushes to Shane

Natasha Shane! Don't let her! Please! I never meant this to happen!

Polly screams out and violently stamps her foot. Silence. Long pause

Wh-what have you done?

Slight pause. Slowly, Natasha goes to Polly. She sees the dead bird

Shane It's dead!

Natasha falls against the satellite dish. Shane rushes to Natasha

Tasha!
Finn (*off*) WHAAATSSGOOINNONUPPAAAIRR?

Everyone freezes

Russell What's that?
Buzz That noise.
Speed I think it's——
Russell Can't be!
Buzz It is!
Speed ⎤ (*together*) Him!
Buzz ⎦
Russell Run!

Russell, Buzz and Speed explode in activity and scarper for the stairs

Finn enters. He is fourteen years old and very large, in all directions, for his age. He is wearing well-worn black jeans, boots, and a T-shirt

*emblazoned with some heavy metal logo, many silver rings and studded
wrist bands. His hair is extremely long and—like the rest of him—in need
of a wash*

Finn WHOOZZMESSINWIIMATELLLE?

Russell, Buzz and Speed yelp, and scarper

Russell The Monster!
Buzz The Monster!
Speed The Monster!

Russell, Buzz and Speed hide

Polly Don't call him that! You'll upset him! It's all right, Finn.
Finn WHAATTEVYYYUNNDOONUPPERRR?
Polly Shhh! Don't worry, Finn. I'll explain.

*Polly whispers in Finn's ear. She points at Jake. Jake gasps. Finn murmurs
and nods. Polly continues whispering in Finn's ear. She points at Natasha.
Natasha gasps. Finn murmurs and nods. Polly continues whispering in
Finn's ear. She points at Carol. Carol gasps. Finn murmurs and nods. Polly
continues whispering in Finn's ear. She points at Russell. Russell cries out.
Finn murmurs and nods. Polly continues whispering in Finn's ear. She
points at Buzz and Speed. They both yell. Finn murmurs and nods. Polly
continues whispering in Finn's ear. She points at Shane. Finn murmurs and
nods. Polly points at herself. Finn's nodding and murmuring get more
emphatic. Polly points at the dead bird. Finn's nodding and murmuring get
even more emphatic. Polly points at Finn. Finn shakes his head, muttering
negatively*

Oh, please, Finn.

Slight pause

Please!

Finn nods and grabs hold of Polly

The Dragon! Help!
Russell The Dragon?
Buzz Him!
Speed He's the Dragon?

Polly Show them, Finn?

Finn claws his hands

Finn RAAAAAGGGHHHHH!!!
All The Dragon!
Russell He's gonna do it!
Finn RAAAAAGGGHHHHH!!!
Polly Help! Help! I've killed what was in the egg. Now the Dragon's kidnapped me for revenge. He's taken me to the top of the mountain. Help! Help!
Natasha It's all my fault!
Russell No, mine!
Carol No, mine!
Jake Mine!
Buzz How's it your fault?
Speed Who are you in all this anyway?
Jake I'm ... her father.

Slight pause

Russell The King!
Carol The one who wouldn't let her grow a flower.
Buzz The one told her to clear off.
Jake That's me!
Speed Then it is your fault!
Russell Where you been all this bloody time?
Jake After what I did to my daughter... I realized I was wrong. I... I was so upset. I hid. Wouldn't show my face. Thought no-one would want to see my face anyway. But then ... then I realized. That wasn't the answer. It just made the problem worse. So now ... now I'm not hiding any more. I'm here to save my daughter. Save her from the Dragon. Is there anyone brave enough to help me?
Russell I will.
Buzz Me too.
Speed And me.
Natasha And me.
Shane And me.
Carol And me.
Buzz What can you do?
Speed You're a bloody nightingale.
Natasha Not any more she's not! Like the King, I'm sorry for what I've done. I've been a bit of a cow really. Let's be friends again—I make you human!

Buzz What about me?
Speed And me.
Shane You too! Human! Human!
Polly Any chance of a bloody rescue!
Jake Arm yourselves!

They rush around finding dustbin lids and other detritus to use as shields and weapons etc. Jake finds an old umbrella to use as a sword. Much noise and activity. Jake stands on an old milk crate. The others gather round him and cheer. They continue to cheer at key moments throughout the following speech

Today we do battle! Battle with a terrible Dragon. A ferocious Dragon. A Dragon with jaws like a shark. A Dragon with scales sharp as razors. A Dragon who glitters bright enough to blind! But a Dragon we must fight! And it's a fight we will win! We'll win because we'll fight it together. Individually—we don't stand a chance. But together—oh, look at us! We are invincible! Are we together?
All Yes!
Jake (*louder*) Are we united?
All (*louder*) Yes!
Jake Then the Dragon is doomed. This Dragon called... Sparkleshark!
All (*chanting*) Sparkleshark! Sparkleshark! Sparkleshark! Sparkleshark!

Everything explodes into action. The chanting is loud and vigorous. Various bits of detritus are used as drums. Jake, Natasha, Carol, Russell, Buzz, Speed and Shane pursue the fleeing Polly and Finn around the roof. Polly is screaming. Finn is roaring. The chanting and general clamour get louder and louder. Everyone, although taking their various roles very seriously, is thoroughly enjoying themselves. Buzz, Speed and Carol help each other over various obstacles etc. Likewise, Shane helps Natasha, and Russell helps Jake. Finally, Finn is surrounded. He lashes out with his clawed hands. Polly watches from one side

Finn RAAAAAGGGHHHHH!!!
Buzz Get him!
Speed Kill him!
Carol (*to Jake*) Save the Princess!

Jake starts to fight Finn. Finn corners Jake. Russell rushes forward

Russell Leave him alone, you son of a bitch!
Jake No, Prince! This is my job! I'm the one who started it all. I must be the one to end it.

Russell But I'm stronger than you!
Finn RAAAAAGGGHHHHH!!!
Russell (*to Jake*) You're right! You do it!

Jake—his umbrella raised—approaches Finn. Finn is roaring and clawing at him. Polly is screaming. The others are avidly cheering Jake on. Suddenly, Finn lashes out at Jake. Jake cries out and falls to the floor. Russell rushes forward and pulls Jake away from Finn

Jake Wh-what are you doing?
Russell The Dragon's broken your arm. You can't carry on. Let me take your sword. Please.

Jake gives Russell the umbrella

Jake Thank you, Prince.
Carol Save the Princess!
Buzz Do it, Prince!
Speed Do it!
Natasha Kill the Dragon.
All (*chanting*) Kill! Kill! Kill! Kill! Kill!

Russell approaches Finn. They circle each other for a while. Everyone cheers, claps, stamps their feet, chants, etc. Finn is clawing at Russell. Russell is swinging the umbrella. They do this in a slow motion, playfully exaggerating every sound and gesture. In the course of the ensuing fight, Russell's umbrella touches Finn's arm. Finn lets out a roar. Then Finn touches Russell's chest. Russell lets out a roar. The crowd continues cheering etc. Finally, Finn is beaten to the ground. Russell raises his umbrella

Kill! Kill! Kill! Kill! Kill!
Russell Die, Sparkleshark! Die!

Then, just as Russell is about to strike——

Polly STOP! (*She rushes to Finn and cradles his head in her lap*)

Everyone is still and silent

This is a good Dragon! A kind Dragon! Yes, I know it kidnapped me. But look what I did. I destroyed its egg! The egg more beautiful than a million yellow flowers.

Pause

And while I've been on this mountain the Dragon has looked after me. Kept me warm at night. Given me food. And I've learned to understand what it's saying.

Finn (*softly*) Raaagghhhaaa.

Polly Yes, my kind Dragon. I'll tell them... Everyone is afraid of him because of what he looks like.

Finn (*softly*) Raaaghhhaaa.

Polly At night, the Dragon spreads its magnificent wings and there's no-one there to marvel how they sparkle by moonlight.

Finn starts to weep. Slight pause

Natasha The Dragon's crying.

Carol Poor Dragon.

Buzz Don't cry.

Speed Don't.

Shane What can we do to stop him crying?

Slight pause

Polly You must lay your hand on the Dragon and say... Oh, tell him you're his friend.

Natasha approaches Finn. She kneels beside him. Lays her hand on him

Natasha I'm your friend, Sparkleshark.

Slight pause. Carol approaches Finn. She kneels beside him. Lays her hand on him

Carol I'm your friend, Sparkleshark.

Slight pause. Buzz approaches Finn. He kneels beside him. Lays his hand on him

Buzz I'm your friend, Sparkleshark.

Slight pause. Speed approaches Finn. He kneels beside him. Lays his hand on him

Speed I'm your friend, Sparkleshark.

Slight pause. Shane approaches Finn. He kneels beside him. Lays his hand on him

Shane I'm your friend, Sparkleshark.

Slight pause. Russell approaches Finn. He kneels beside him. Lays his hand on him

Russell I'm your friend, Sparkleshark.

Slight pause. Jake approaches Finn. He kneels beside him. Lays his hand on him

Jake I'm your friend, Sparkleshark.

Slight pause

Finn Raaahhh.
Polly Sparkleshark is your friend too.

Pause. Jake stands

Jake And, from that moment on, the land could live in perfect peace. The Prince and Princess lived happily in their Castle. The Wizard and the Witch created new planets together. The one-time horses, Thunder and Lightning, became best friends with the one-time frog and nightingale. I—the King—was forgiven. And, at night, if children saw a strange light in the sky, their parents would say, "Don't worry, my love. That's just moonlight on the Dragon's wings."

Long, silent pause. Polly begins to applaud Jake. The others join in to various degrees. All except Russell who moves away from the group

But it wasn't just me! It was all of us! Together! The story—it belongs to all of us.
Polly Let's do another one! Jake!
Carol I'm up for that.
Buzz Me too.
Speed And me.
Jake I'd like to but ... well, I've got to get home for tea.

Slight pause

Polly But ... we can't just stop there! Natasha?
Natasha We could meet again. Shane?
Shane ...If you want.

Carol Next week!
Buzz Same time!
Speed Same place!
Polly We should call ourselves something!
Natasha Like a group—yes! Of course!

Slight pause

Buzz ...The Storytelling Group!
All (*except Russell*) Nah! That's terrible! (*Etc.*)

Slight pause

Speed The SAS—Secret Association of Storytellers.
All (*except Russell*) Nah! That's even worse! (*Etc.*)
Finn ...Sparkleshark!

Slight pause

Polly Yes, Finn! That's it! We'll call ourselves "Sparkleshark"! Jake?
Jake Sounds good to me.
Shane ...And me.
All (*except Russell*) Yeah! Sparkleshark!
Jake And ... we'll have a salute! Our secret sign. For when we meet each
   other—the Dragon's claw. (*He claws his fist as Finn had done*)
   Sparkleshark!

They all—except Russell—punch the air with the salute

All (*all except Russell*) Sparkleshark!

They all—except Russell—climb up the metal staircase to the raised platform

Jake (*punching the air with the salute*) Sparkle... (*He notices Russell below*)

Slight pause

Buzz What's wrong, Russ?
Speed What, Russ?
Russell It's bloody stupid.
Carol No! It's not!
Polly You enjoyed it too.
Russell I forgot myself. That's all.

Polly Well, you found something better.

Russell Life ain't a bloody fairytale. There's no happy ever after. I know.

Natasha You think I don't?

Carol We're not bloody stupid.

Polly We're not talking happy ever after, Russ. We're talking ... just this once.

Russell But ... it don't change anything, Pol.

Natasha It could.

Carol It might.

Natasha Who knows?

Polly Just ... just do the Sparkleshark salute with us.

Carol It feels good. Tell him, you two.

Buzz It does, Russ.

Speed Yeah, Russ.

Natasha Oh, tell him, Shane.

Shane ...Feel it! Just once!

Slight pause. Russell hovers between staying where he is and rushing to join them. He wants to resist them. And yet... And yet... Suddenly, Russell rushes for the stairs. The others cheer him on. Russell joins them on the platform. Then, suddenly and simultaneously, they all punch the air with the clawed salute

All (*triumphantly*) SPARKLESHARK!

Black-out

FURNITURE AND PROPERTY LIST

Further dressing may be added at the director's discretion

On stage: Many TV aerials and satellite dishes
Discarded household furniture
Piles of rubbish and various scattered detritus
Old armchair
Dead bird
Supermarket trolley
Old shoe
Old baseball cap
Old lampshade
Dustbin lids
Old umbrella
Milk crate

Off stage: Satchel containing notebook (**Jake**)
Tiny tool box containing screwdriver (**Polly**)
Very full sports bag (**Buzz**)
2 very full sports bags. *In one of them*: football (**Speed**)
Handbag covered with gold sequins. *In it*: perfume, lipstick, face compact, hairclip (**Natasha**)

Personal: **Jake**: glasses, pen
Polly: several folded sheets
Carol: gold handbag
Shane: razorblade necklace, sunglasses

LIGHTING PLOT

Property fittings required: nil
1 exterior. The same throughout

To open: Sunny autumn afternoon lighting

Cue 1   **All:** "Sparkleshark!"   (Page 39)
            Black-out

EFFECTS PLOT

*No cue*s